WISH TO REACH THE SUMMIT

USHERING HAPPINESS

MRINAL KANTI GUIN

ISBN 979-888606265-6

Kali Sadhan Guin, My Father he who motivate me to reach the summit.

Contents

Contents

Preface

Wish to reach the summit

We are born on the earth and gradually grown up with the passage of time. Everyone gets education as much as he or she can. Parents and relatives live with us since childhood as result of which there is no problem with us. The problem starts when we realize that this society expects a lot from us too. We know that the burden of our society or country will be in the hands of this young people of this country. It will be our sacred duty to lead that youth community in the right direction with the passage of time. The future of a secure country can be expected only from them. The youth of this country has to move forward slowly but steadily. They should not be broken down into pieces with small or minor hurdle. They should be stronger than the lightning with a speed higher than the light

Disappointment must be thrown out from today. They should be more and more energetic. They should not be broken down into pieces from failures. As a natural phenomenon, failure will come as a stepping stone towards the ultimate success. Every task should have a deadline. They should have planned accordingly to complete them within given deadline.

It should be bear in mind that none has ever left to anyone without leaving a single point during any types of competition. In this connection, one of the sentences of Duryodhana in the Mahabharata is very relevant in which he said to the Pandavas - "Without any type of war I will not let you any soil of this kingdom."

In the real world, though, it is true. No one leaves anything to anyone. It is to be achieved in true sence. He who achieves wins at the last. At the end there is no room for guilt or frustration from this knowledge.

So you have to put more effort and work harder again and again until the goal is achieved.

Sometimes frustration comes; it is quite natural, nothing wrong in it. There are some people everywhere who do nothing but discourage everyone in various ways. There should have no room to break down easily and if so, they become in the list of the failures. The mind has to be as energetic, courageous and determined as a lion, the king of the jungle.

With a lot of hope, I started writing a book this year.

It is especially written for the purpose of the youth of the country. I have seen that they need to be focused in the right direction. Young men and women of this age get easily frustrated which is not good for the country or the nation at all.

If my effort in this regard is of any use to anyone, I will be blessed.

This will be my most ambitious book of 2022.

Take care, Thank you

Mrinal Kanti Guin

Dated:-31.01.2022

CHAPTER ONE

Plan: The overview at a glance

When we are very young, we are loved by everyone. In this way one day, I become grown up according to the infallible rules of the universe. We have started a rat race since early days of our school. Many parents nowadays consider their children as an investment item. It must be remembered here that there is a class of people who consider that the education should be compulsory and they should take more important decisions in it. They have to spend a lot of money every month to get their children enrolled in a good school or academy.

The Constitution of India has made education compulsory for all children of this country. For this reason, the RTE Act has been enacted and implemented nicely throughout the entire country. In case some other country, similar type of action has been taken long ago or may be taken in day's to come. Many developed counrties like USA, Japan, France, UK etc. have already taken such types initiative since long ago. As a result of which, they are harnessing the good result for those initiatives. It is needless to say that the literacy percentage of those developed nations are comparatively very high. There is no doubt that this has greatly improved the child's education at this point of time. Along with government-sponsored educational institutions, private educational institutions also play a very significant role in this regard. Many private institutions throughout the world are now pioneering in the field of education, research and development. They lend their hand not only for the business for earning money but also for the human resource development at a large. The society has, at this point, being benefitted from those holistic approach.

At the same time, education has spread in the schools. Today the rate of education in India has increased considerably and the problem has arisen right here. Billions of students are passing through the campus year after year after getting their desired degree. Everyone should keep a record of the various aspects that have been opened up at present. We have to adapt ourselves to the age with static wisdom. In English it is called adaptation or adaptation to the age. A perfect case of brain drain is also happening through out the world for more or less amount of job seeker who sometimes hanker after higher wages, facility and in many case of working environment.

From prehistoric times, we have seen that those who have not been able to adapt have gradually disappeared from the earth. The largest example of a widely studied dinosaur but that contemporary cockroach is still alive in this earth with great vigour.

If we look at the modern age, many things may come to our mind. Such as the case of Kodak Film Company and Nokia Mobile Company. Did anyone think this fate of those great multinational companies as they are today? Off course, not. So, think every aspect very deeply. Anything may come out anytime which may bring excellant benefit to the mankind

It will continue to do so in the future also. If we do not improve ourselves, the first thing that happens is that we lose our importance at the point of our work. Even after that, if we do not change ourselves, we will become insignificant to this world. Will it be a great honour for us? Certainly not at all.

Can you tell why private companies hire these useless and worthless fellow workers? To survive in this age fierce competition, companies will certainly take some innovative steps to reduce production costs with the higher quality improvement. If necessary, they reduce the number of such useless workers who are considered as the burden of the company. Well, tell me, who will keep them at the expense of their valuable resource?

The answer of the question can be given by even a common man and off course, very easily, there is no need to be an expert. So do not stay in the imaginary world. Keep learning; learn something new every day that will definitely work for you in the future. Get rid of the sense immediately that you know everything. The sooner you get out of that shell of ignorance, the better it will be. Don't get in trouble with anyone without any cause. Well, this may not hurt anyone else; your own loss is inevitable.

So avoid any type of trouble as much possible as you can, it will undoubtedly increase the efficiency of your thinking process in your brain. Undoubtedly, you will be far ahead of your competitor in this regard. Make your speech as short as possible. Say less and listen more. If possible, say goodbye to any type of emotions. Avoid associating unnecessary people as much as possible. If you can do this, you will see that you have saved a lot of your valuable time. Take advantage of that saved time. Remember that the time that is being neglected today never comes back again. If we do not use this valuable time as resource of time properly, no one has the power to achieve any type of success. Miracle does not happen by chance in one's life, it has to make it happen. Always bear in mind-" Time and tide wait for none." Come out from the shell of ignorance and lend your bold hand to the achievement of mankind.

CHAPTER TWO

The goal of life: The ultimate desire

" The goal of life should be clearly defined, it is extremely important to every individual "

We all fall in love with so many things at once. As a result, our real target becomes secondary to many things or objects or persons. The goal of life should never be imaginary, it should be well defined and achievable for the individual after certain amount of time and effort. The energy that the God has given to our body spreads in different directions if the goal is not rightly set at that point of time. So even if we hope for success in our minds, that success does not come in time in proper manner. So, don't take it lightly. A well defined goal of life is certainly play a better role in that person's way to success.

That is a fact of life. So first of all we should set a target or goal in life. It is inevitable to learn by looking at this subject but it is not right to imitate. If we imitate, the success will not be achieved at all and our desired result shall be a big zero which is not acceptable by the society.

We all know that the Creator in this universe has endowed everyone with infinite power, so we should always be grateful to Him. However, it should be remembered that the talents of all human beings are not equal. Those people who are considered equally important need to think about their own lives first than think for the society. it is needless to point out that person with higher intelligence achieve all desired result in quite ease but others also may achieve the desired success if they become relentlessly try to succeed for a quite a long period of time. If so, everything is seem to be achievable by everyone. It is quite obvious for the human beings. So don't loose heart, try, try, and try again.

Don't make any decisions based on your emotions or previous experience. Emotion is a heavenly fellings so its use should be limited olny. Don't give your passion to everyone or tell them everything because sometimes they are not all worthy of your invaluable and indomitable passion. This will definitely reduce the wastage of your time and energy. It is very important feeling to consider for your success.

So make the most of your time and energy by setting goals first. Stick to it and watch it's advancement regularly from time to time, if you do this, you will be successful one day. This is guaranteed.

Failure should/may come first. Our experience is that most of the time when failure comes, don't break down but to increase the effort more wisely. One day success will come. It is cent true in all the cases.

It is good to have more memories, but those who say "memory is always happy" will see that they are always in the past and they can't do anything good in the future. It is pessimistic thought. So throw the monster called memory that weakens us in the dustbin of the mind. This is simply garbage. Don't even look at them.

Come to the ground of reality, most of the people in the memory are not with you today and in the past you have never been in reality and in the future you will never be. So don't waste your precious time and energy thinking about these utterly nonsense.

You are also an important person in this world. You can give a lot to the world so you have to come forward first.

To think of oneself as insignificant is tantamount to suicide. So don't think too much about it. Don't discuss your decision with too many people or go for advice.

This is because most of them do not have the ability to give that great advice and many of those who think they have it do not want to improve your mind and this will not serve your business. This is surely not good for your future even.

Be careful every time, be happy always, spend more and more time with family and close friends. Away from unnecessary debates, always keep the fire of determination for success in your mind. You will see, success is just a matter of time.

CHAPTER THREE

Concentration: The full cause

Every human brain has a certain capacity. It is unfortunate that only a few percent of it we can use during our life. As per the world famous scientist Einstein is especially noteworthy here. He said, "I know how much of this world there is ? We walk on the beach of sands and sometimes took out some glittering sand as which may be considered as knowledge."

See, how much the humility is! Think about it carefully. So if we think we can achieve success by acquiring all the knowledge in the world, there can be no greater foolishness than that. So we should focus on one thing at a time in this small life. This greatly increases the chances of success. Because of this,

1) It increases the efficiency of your brain. It is always easier to remember the result of one kind of thinking. This is because it increases the function of the frontal lobe of the brain. We can remember it everything easily through this process.

2) It also saves a lot of time. As a result, more and more time is needed to get the right idea.

3) When different things are brought to the brain at the same time, different types of thoughts come and which eventually increases mental stress in single point of time. It can lead to outbreak of various types of diseases including high blood pressure or hypertension. They many deviate you from your goal. We know - "Health is an asset." Those who do not have proper health and physique, even if they have the depth of knowledge, cannot be easily appreciated in the society and can not able to deliver the service in time, and the people at large will not rely on the sick person. It is also noeworthy to mentain that why the society will depend on such uncertainty? It is risky for the people at a large. So this issue is primarily considered as much very important.

4) Once the goal of one's life is decided, well defined and configured as future , that should be considered as the biggest thing and live dream in life. It is important to consider it as a bird's eye view until it is fulfilled. Single point agenda, that is! That's why you always need to build yourself up to get it first. So, train your mind for that reason.

5) If you practice on the same subject again and again, as the skill increases as the time passes, so does the strength of mind or self-confidence. The success rate multiplied unquestionably. Pour all the unsolved questions into one busket. Solve them one by one with dignity and peace of mind. Don't left anyone and anything untouched and unnoticed.

6) If you practice one thing and keeping pace with the times, the improvement of your life is inevitable and will be unquestionable. One day you will see that there is no one beside you because you are already far ahead of others in respect of success. You will soon see the face of success in

new places. Try practicing success and good news on it's way in near future

Success is followed.

CHAPTER FOUR

Learn to say no!

The more we improve, the more selfish we become. Our demand is now increasing day by day. We are working hard to meet all those needs more wisely. The problem is more here. Extra money falls into the hands of a class of people. Don't say in words - "Money pulls money." The matter is incredibly true. One class of people is getting richer day by day. Another class of people is becoming fossils day by day and they become poorer as the time advances. Those who shout about humanity are busy packing their own sugarcane. It was at that time that the greatest humiliation of humanity took place. The protector of humanity becomes the biggest eater as a result of which the situation worsen more and more day by day. Just then the biggest curse in the life of an innocent person comes down heavily, which become truly unbearable to them.

Arrogant people turn red with shame in disguise.

A class of people has extra important responsibilities and another class of people is starting to end up in a hurry. This perishable class of people will one day die if they do not take appropriate action at the right time.

They are used blatantly for free day by day by the other class of people. This class of people has less talk. They have been used for free in other people's work for ages. Many times without any remuneration. As a result they become poorer day by day. It often takes the form of a vicious cycle

In general, this class of people is more humane and they are used by other classes day by day without any compensation.

So when you realize that you are being misused by another class, learn to tell them right away. If you think that you will get something in return in the near future then that is nothing but stupidity. The ways in which this class of people fools the other class are:

1) Acting of love, - A class of clever women do this acting very smoothly. They choose innocent cowboy type boys for this. Day after day they use it for their own work and just cut it when needed. When the poor fellow understands, he can pass. So in this case you should always step very carefully instantly.

2) Promise to help in the future, - In this case, it is necessary to move carefully from all classes of people. Unethical people often treat you that way. Keep your eyes and ears open a little. You can understand that. When you understand this person's intentions or bad intentions, leave that person's relationship immediately. The sooner you can do this, the better.

3) The person who benefits from this - be the most careful of this class of people. This is especially true for women. You will see a class of men irrelevantly coming or going to benefit you. In this case, ask yourself a question. You will get the right answer.

4) There is another class of people who never look for you. They look for you when they need you. That class of people are terribly selfish. If you know them, say no immediately to them. It is foolish to expect help from this class of people.

This is not to say that people should not be helped. Of course people need help but it is very important that you say no to the person who is unjustly harming you and using you repeatedly in his work with unjust or false promises.

You will benefit from this. You will save a lot of time. At this time you can use your work to improve yourself.

A smart person but never straightforwardly said "no". When they recognize these greedy people, they do such things that the person does not even come near them.

Therefore, the expression of the mind should be expressed in a smooth manner. The snake dies and the stick does not break.

So don't make the mistake of recognizing people. Appreciate a good person. Say goodbye to others with appropriate feedback.

CHAPTER FIVE

No substitute for education

There is a saying- "Learn as long as live." There is no need to discuss the matter in details. We all know it, but we may not realize it, so we don't believe it. Those who do not understand - they have to pay the price step by step for this, some understand and some do not understand.

The matter can be better understood by giving an example.

Two person in an area started a business from same point of time. One of the two is a truly businessman and another like earn his livlihood only.

The two started a business side by side at the same time about forty years ago. The two of them spend all day in that business. Today, one of them is still sitting with that capital he started. There was no remarkable development in his business. Only somehow he has spent the family. Another businessman, however, has improved a lot. His business has grown remarkably. He has now hired a few employees to help with his work. He also pays remuneration to the employees on time. As a result, the family of his employees is doing well.

We can analyse the situation of two person in a detail through a case study.

Why is that? In reality, there are so many examples, if you notice a little. You can find such examples everywhere. Analysis shows the mentality of those two people along with the position they are now holding. It is quite obvious. You will see that one has always focused on one's own experience or education and has increased it silently day by day. Day by day that education has been put to use in their business. He has done all this in a very honest and timely manner. He has increased his skills day by day. He was never satisfied with his education. If necessary, he has worked harder day after day. He then successfully applied his skills. He has also increased the skills of his employees if needed. Besides, it is good to see his personal conduct and he is planning far-reaching. Good use and successful implementation of good plans always bring more benefits to all people.

That is to say, you and you alone are responsible for wherever you are today.

Even if someone is very rich, he is responsible. The same is true for the poor.

The one who has withdrawn or is keeping himself away from this teaching will have to pay the price one day. Be it today or a few days later.

This is especially true for those candidates who are currently preparing for the examination to get job. They need to keep in mind that no matter what school you went to as a child or no matter how many marks you secured, you have to start studying again from scratch. Always remember, studying for securing high marks in school examination is never the same as studying for a job. However, many of those who have studied well as students are getting a lot of extra benefits. That, of course, is true.

In a word, there is no substitute for regular education and regular perseverance.

In short, there is no shortcut in learning which ultimately leads into grand success.

CHAPTER SIX

The right book: The beginning of road

There is saying - "If you want to cure any disease, you need to take the right medicine at the right time in the right amount."

Besides, it is necessary to visit to the doctor to cure the disease. These words are true. We have all been listening to it with fascination and we have been following it for ages.

There are many well-known books on the market, and many well-known authors have written them in different ways. Various kinds of thoughts of science, literature, art, etc. are embedded in these books. They are a timeless creation for the ages. They have been providing light to mankind for ages. The book has made them immortal and invincible through the ages.

All books are based on one or the other subject matter. There is no special purpose in composing them.

Every scripture provides some specific lesson in human life. The reader needs to know what he wants before choosing that book.

Therefore, there is a special need to decide on the demand by analyzing the correct judgment first. To be sure, it is important to collect one or more of the best books on the subject. That selection will bring about a radical change in you or your family. It's just a matter of time.

I personally believe that every book or text will have a timely effect on your life no matter what you say. So the right choice is very important.

Then they must be studied with devotion. The more devoted a person is in this regard, the sooner he will get those benefits.

The advice of an experienced person should be taken for choosing this book as it makes your job much easier. Everyone's participation in this competition of life is inevitable. So do not sit with folded hands. Take part in this great struggle of life and make history by winning.

Every human brain function increases on the use of his brain. No one can stop you from winning if you have self-confidence.

You have to overcome inertia and work for the betterment of your life. In this case, there is a class of omniscient people who are busy packing their own luggage, they are timid by sense. Don't go to them. They are more harmful than venomous snakes. They are selfish, violent, vampire and hell worms. Be away from all these disgusting people thousands miles. It will definitely improve you as well as people from all walks of life.

CHAPTER SEVEN

Knowledge: Its' depth

Before we start any work we should think of everything first and then start working. After thinking about it, it is easier for you to decide which way to go. Then we have to move on to its consequences.

This has been discussed in detail in the previous chapter.

After I have done all those things, I have to build myself irresistible, unrivaled. In this case, having the slightest doubt in any corner of the mind is detrimental to all aspects of life.

Need to study proper textbooks. If necessary, it should be read again and again. Then you have to write about these things and practice again and again. You will feel that a different force of mind has enriched your mind. The force of this mind, but not at all, is invaluable. In many cases it comes too early and in some cases it is too late. But in the case of every person, it can be said with certainty that the force of this mind will take you to a peak of progress.

Also, if necessary, like-minded people can be discussed. This discussion or debate should be constructive criticism no matter what it is called. There is no doubt that everyone will benefit greatly from this. When certain subjects are studied, 100 percent care should be taken of all kinds of questions that may come up on that subject or topic. Doing any kind of haste in this regard will not work at all. You just have to be more discriminating with the help you render toward other people. That time is very private. Don't let anyone in the world come to you at that time. That means you have to give yourself time honestly. This is true not only for those who are preparing themselves for competition but also for all people in the world. Those who adhere to it gradually reach the pinnacle of improvement day by day.

One should find time for oneself only. In that specified time nobody should be allowed to disturb. In that time he or she should use that time for their personal development. It is a step by step learning process. It is a continuous and very much useful process.

Is there any doubt that if a person adheres to it properly, he will get very good result if there is any question about that knowledge during the test? And if any person can do it successfully, he will surely be in a very high position in the society.

Everything should be learnt in depth, there is no place of improper knowledge.. There is a saying " Little learning is a dangerous thing!"

CHAPTER EIGHT

Reading habits: Its' methodology

We all know that the scope of knowledge in this world is so great that it is not possible for anyone to evaluate it properly. So history goes by and we often see around us that the less knowledgeable people often sit in higher positions and the more knowledgeable people arc forced to spend their whole lives from the very bottom.

We can find out the reason in a little more detail. The thing that comes to our notice is that the results of any of our competitive examinations are not at all an assessment of his personal merit. The result is the best among the candidates who have written well always placed in higher position. In this world, a person is evaluated in this transient way.

I personally do not support this approach. It doesn't matter if we accept it or not.

So in this momentary way of searching for merit, if you want to see the face of success, you can get a lot of good results by adopting a few methods.

First of all, we have to remember that there are three types of study throughout our life.

1) Schooling:

It basically extends from childhood to university. This is how our academic career is made. Which is obvious necessary for us to choose different types of professions in the future.

2) Subject based or action based study:

This type of study relies heavily on school-based learning. If you want to see the face of success in most cases, you have to study more deeply. This type of study has also become institutionalized in the current competition in various fields. At present, various organizations are imparting education to various job seekers through such educational institutions. They, normally, do not offer any degree. They make job seekers more proficient through training and practice. Many job seekers have succeeded using this and have got an economic and a social establishment in life.

3) Education for knowledge:

It sounds a lot like a golden stone bowl. To know all the lessons in a real way: In the first case, the degree is available. In the second case, for earning . In the third case, none of this is available, but there is endless peace of mind. In this the scope of knowledge increases unquestionably. New life is revealed. Extreme development occurs in all aspects of human ideas. Mental development occurs which is very important and useful for the human race.

In order to survive in the battle of life, people have to get acquainted with new sciences every day, otherwise they have to remain behind which is often not very prestigious. The person who looks back once is thought to have deteriorated. The one who always wants to come forward, will see that he is always awake and has made sure that he is an expert in all other matters.

There are ten types of study methods. They are briefly discussed here.

I) SQ3R method:

In this way the students are made to understand the important points of the book. In this method the whole process is divided into five steps. They are very relevant.

A) Survey

In this case, instead of reading the whole book, the important information of each chapter is found and they are recorded differently.

B) Question

What we learned from the chapter and what questions might come up are written down.

C) Read

Then we have to write the answers to all those questions from the whole chapter.

D) Recite

After studying, you need to change these into your own language and think of important information.

E) Review

You have to memorize the chapter or make it interesting by doing quizzes etc. If necessary, the important thing should be better understood once again.

II) Retrieval Practice :

Once read, read for a while ,the subject must be read again. It also tests how much you remember. In this way the students have to recall the important points of the book. As a result, the subject becomes better understood and the subject becomes deeply ingrained in the mind.

This is practiced repeatedly by continuing the experiment. If you create that question by yourself and write the answer yourself and what I wrote, it will be matched with the original text and you will have to take a plan to improve the quality of the answer. If necessary, the answer is corrected again by consulting the original book..

Flashcards are used here. The cards are hung on the wall of the study room. The short answer to the question is written below. So there is no need to open the book all the time.

III) Spaced Practice :

In this way students have to concentrate on the same subject for a long time. It is time dependent. This method is very effective if it can be planned in advance. This method plays an effective role behind the merit of meritorious students.

It creates an idea in the mind. As a result, there is no need to remember. I think everything just stays with you.

In this method students have to remember a few steps

The first day - things have to go well.

Day 2 - You have to re-read that subject and understand it well.

Third day - you have to read it again and again and understand it well.

After a week - will have to read and understand again.

After two weeks - read again and see if you remember everything. The possibility of assimilation is very strong.

IV) PQ4R method:

This method tries to remember things in six steps.

Preview - A general idea is formed by flipping through the pages of a book to get an idea of what the subject is before reading it.

After that the whole chapter is read and the answers to these questions are found. Then it is seen again (Reflect) whether all the questions have been answered? Then they are studied well in their own language (Recite). The last step is to see (Review) all the things I know if you remember!

V) Feynman method:

What I learned from studying a subject is to write it down first. Then it is described in its own language. Then it is necessary to examine from the original text how relevant what is written is. The ones that are wrong have to be corrected again.

This method is most effective for teachers.

VI) Leitner's method:

It seemed to be very subject based and complex. This method is used for reading through flashcards. The practice is not discussed as complicated.

VII) Color-Code-Note:

It uses different colored inks on the book. These colored leaves increase the efficiency of the brain and that method especially affects human life.

VIII) Mind Mapping :

In this case, instead of reading, the subject is seen in pictures or videos. Through this the subject is easily remembered. Nowadays that method is very popular, especially for young children. In this way the internal development of children's brain is very good.

IX) Exercise before studying:

Many times it is seen that the content is not understood properly due to inertia. So, if you can turn around a little or exercise a little empty hand to study continuously, then you will be able to overcome the inertia of the mind.

X) Study before bed:

If you study before going to bed, the memories often come back to you in your sleep and take place in your mind forever. Researchers at York University in England have found that our brains produce a kind of memory that we read before we go to sleep. So the things that are read before going to sleep, if everyone practices them again, it becomes long lasting.

In conclusion, whether we know it or not, we follow all these methods completely or partially. Scientists have tested and found that if all people adhered to those methods well, they would be greatly improved. There is no room for doubt in it.

CHAPTER NINE

Mental strength: It's effectivity

A person becomes what he thinks he is. It is universal truth. I ersonally experinced it. It is really a great deal for the present as well as in near future. This requires a great deal of self-sacrifice, self tolerence and off course perseverance. The more successful a person is in life, the more he can be seen by looking at the history of that person. In other words, he has become pure by burning in different fires of the society. Here we will discuss about how to enhance one's personality. And we generally think that some people are born with God's blessing. I will discuss them. I will know the details of why or how they received such blessings.

Are they people of another world! No, I will know that like ten ordinary people.

For this we need the help of science. We all know that if we do what we like to do, we do it in a very good way. It makes our body and mind very good. And that's exactly where the problem lies. Most of the time we do what we like and if we do that we will do better in the future - not at all.

So it should be good to do what will be good in the future. If these two cases are combined then no one can stop the future improvement of that person. His prosperity gradually increased.

And if what he likes doesn't work out well in the future, then he should think differently on a personal level.

Many of us know why we love a particular thing. Why do we love to do something special?

Because we get used to doing a lot of what we love to do. Again, I love what I get used to doing. A kind of organic matter is responsible for this. This substance, called dopamine, is secreted from our brain. The more we love to do, the more dopamine is secreted. If one loves to study, then dopamine is secreted while studying. The matter is very auspicious in the case of that person. There is no doubt that he will reach the peak of improvement day by day in his life.

The problem is that there are times when the person loves something that will not only improve in the future but also cause harm. For example, a person is addicted to gambling. In this case, his dopamine is released during gambling. In this case if proper treatment is not done then day by day that person will go to the abyss. So the family needs to be aware enough before taking any kind of bad drug. Otherwise bad intoxication माँ becomes an obstacle to the person's progress. The situation is not at all pleasant for any family members. Which direction the child will go depends a lot on the activities of the family members.

Many times proper treatment or counseling can revive such people from many dangers. So when the problem arises, do not sit idly by. If necessary, we have to take this important decision.

In another case, we can improve ourselves. We can start practicing what is good for the future. For example, getting into the habit of reading books. In this case, if a job seeker can turn studies into an addiction, he will one day be engaged in a good profession. Day by day he continues to improve his life. Once his preparation reaches such a height, it becomes invaluable to the job seeker. So the key to success is nowhere else, success comes on your own honest efforts, hard work and concentration.

Don't pay attention to nonsense, the role of this concentration is immense and essential. Walk these slowly to feel calm. You will see that God is always with you. Do not hate anyone. It costs a lot to hate and the memory of our brain. Unnecessary head heat also has an adverse effect on concentration.

Be humble: it is rewarding to all. It is tested. It is everlasting and also gave compounding benefit for the person who practise it with full attention.

Relationships: Key to success

Every human being survives because human beings are social beings. After the birth of a small child, he grows up in the company of his family. His education began slowly. Both parents pass on their ideals to their children knowingly or unknowingly. All these relationships are oxygen to the children. There is no way people can live without it. There are also some social relationships such as teachers, friends, companions, etc. They have nothing to do with blood relation, yet those people play an important role in our lives. Not only are they involuntarily involved in our lives but much of our life depends on them. Kids rely a lot on their friends when they grow up. So a lot depends on who the kids will hang out with. In this case, there is a lot of responsibility on the parents. They should keep in mind that their children's brain structure largely depends on the activities of their peers. So it is very important to keep a close eye on who the children are associating with. Not only this, with the help of fire you can do welding.

In addition to the healthy development of the child's brain should be taken care of. For this they need to be given proper education as well as good reforms. As a result, that child will one day become a good citizen. That is what all the parents as well as the people of our society and country expect. Children should be educated from the beginning to build a well-educated and organized society. Sadly, this is true of many parents today who start a rat race to increase their children's brain function. As a result, child-friendly agility is suppressed by artificial learning. It can be the opposite of hi-tech. As a result, instead of being good citizens, these children became violent, jealous, spineless citizens. But if they were given proper education at the right time, then their opinion would have developed enough. As a result, the country, society and family would inevitably benefitted. There is saying- "Charity begins at home."

Many people think that children should not be allowed to associate with anyone at an early age because the child's brain does not know what is good and what is bad. Although this thinking is proven to be correct in many cases, children need an open environment for the normal and holistic development of the brain. The best way to educate yourself is to encourage them to do something good from the bottom of their hearts.

The future of the children depends a lot on the parents. It should always be well thought out. It should also be kept in mind that when children grow up, they have to be left alone, as they become acquainted with all kinds of people in the society, which plays a very important role in shaping life. Parents need to understand that they will not live forever. Everyone has to survive alone in the jungle called this world.

After growing up, it is seen that a group of students is formed naturally. "Birds with the same feather flock together." These words are very effective at this time. So choosing a partner at this time has an important effect in the future. If all the partners have deep dreams or hopes in their minds, then everyone can easily implement their own life goals. In this case they can do group study, group discussion very easily. They will be considered very important for everyone.

CHAPTER ELEVEN

Food habit: My strength

Much depends on our experience or body language. The experience increases day by day with age. So in the light of this experience, it is often fun to learn a lot. You will know a lot of unknown information even after reading a lot of time.

It is especially important to discuss our main topic of eating and drinking here. The matter of assimilation is a very complex process. So here is a small idea should be there of what happens when you take which type of food.

Basically we divide this food into two parts. The first is where we can't produce any energy but they are essential for our body. These are minerals as well as some elements like iron, sodium, potassium, magnesium, iodine. These enter our body through various compounds. Different types of vitamins are needed in appropriate amounts in our body. Vitamins A, B complex, C, D, E, K, H etc. All these vitamins help the various elements in the body to function properly. As a result, they help maintain a healthy body. Health is wealth. It is very important thing for consideration of future. Therefore, proper eating habits and proper amount of sleep at the right time play a vital role in the health of the body.

Foods that produce energy are carbohydrates, fats, proteins. We all know that there are 4.2 K calories from sugar, protein and 9.2 K calories from fat. So it is very important to eat right amount at the right time.

Many times we eat different types of vegetables, fruits and from them we get almost everything. Different types of pulses including fish, meat and eggs meet our daily protein needs. Rice, bread is considered as an example of carbohydrate. From them we get the energy we need in our daily lives. Different types of oil, ghee or animal fatty foods meet our fat needs. If we consider them as the simplest then glucose, fatty acids and amino acid foods. That food enters our body in a complex form. Our body breaks down that complex food into simple through various enzymes. The process by which this whole process takes place is called digestion. This whole process is completed outside the living cell.

Then the intercellular process begins. This is known as metabolism. But there are two types of metabolism. They are anabolism and catabolism. This metabolism normally takes place in the mitochondria of the cell and we get a lot of energy from ADP by making ATP. So we can't waste this endless energy in vain. Think about what is created through such a complex process, that energy should always be used for good deeds themselves or for social development.

CHAPTER TWELVE

Making fun or great personality!

Everyone has a childhood dream in their life to become something when they grow up. Does it ever match the picture of reality? We know the reason for such mismatch. There are so many sacrifices behind growing up. This sacrifice is not only his own but family members also. Many times self-sacrifice are in the form of money, ease and many times or invaluable something else. This small sacrifice of life often becomes very big in the mind of the child. They help to nurture the baby properly later on. In the mind of a small child, many small things can be seen growing up. So before using it with children, you must think and talk. Before deciding on this, one should think about various psychological issues of the child.

Some of the things that provide momentary pleasure in the present may not bode well for the future. So we have to make the right decision about these. We have to choose between the momentary happiness or the bright future because the bright future gives the direction of so many pieces of happiness. So all those decisions should be taken very carefully. Big decisions, if taken at the right time, pay off.

Many of us have seen many school and college classmates drowning in madness or in day dream. I myself was disappointed many times to see them! After a while I thought about the future in a cold head, then I realized that they are not doing the right thing at all. Do what you think! Today, they are lost in the current of the bottom! Their madness at that time was very cheap. Then it was time to study, then they cheated there, now it is their turn to count the toll on their interest.

So what we are doing now will pay off in the future. If you do good work, you will get good results! And if you do bad things today -

So you should choose the one that will make your future better.

The choice is open to all, all the time and you have to choose the right one which suits for you the best for the future. The choice is yours.

Manytime different paradigm shift are happening in our life cycle, it is quite natural for a living being. An individual, after fulfilment of a particular target, can and should set another target and so on. So, for a target or goal oriented person, his or her life always become a place of worship for future. Many individual take this oppertunity and some others makes it a fun for future.

Be a single individual, always cherish what your mind remains. Hope is gold and dream is a real dimond for future.

CHAPTER THIRTEEN

Mitochondria: The power house

Let's think a little differently today. Let's discuss science in a little detail. We often deliberately bow to superstition and heresy without the application of any thought. Read on to find out where our mistake is! Then I blushed with shame.

One of the things we often hear is that if you don't have a son, you don't have a family. In this regard, it can be said with gene theory that out of twenty-three pairs of human chromosomes, twenty-two pairs of autosomes and one pair of sex chromosomes. A pair of chromosomes determines sex. That is, it determines whether the child will be a boy or a girl. The sex determining chromosomes are the X and Y chromosomes. If the union of XX then the child will be a girl and if the union of XY then the child will be a boy. All of these chromosomes contain a substance called DNA. So if the child is a boy or a girl, it is decided by the father. Not at all by mom.

Besides, many of us may not know that there is DNA in a place other than the nucleus. That is mitochondria. This DNA is round. In this mitochondria all the energy is released from the food we eat. All these complex functions are performed by making ATP and ADP.

Well, tell me, where does this mitochondrial DNA come from? From father or mother?

Surprisingly, this DNA comes from the mother. Not from the father at all.

Look at the irony of nature, father determines gender and mother produces energy. So many times mother is considered as the source of extreme energy. What could be the scientific release of this? From our experience and scientific knowledge we know that neither mother nor father, son or daughter is complete by itself. That mystery of nature has not yet been fully revealed. Science and scientists are unraveling that mystery by unveiling new horizons.

Where our knowledge is limited today, it will expand in the coming days through the revelation of new things. That is why it is so important to encourage everyone at all times. So, judging by heredity, no parent is inferior to anyone. Therefore, those old patriarchal ideas should be eradicated immediately and thrown in the dustbin. This will lead to the development of people from all walks of life.

CHAPTER FOURTEEN

Socrates: Good enough

i) "The only true wisdom is in knowing you know nothing."

ii) "The unexamined life is not worth living."

iii) "I cannot teach anybody anything.

iv) "There is only one good, knowledge, and one evil, ignorance."

v) "Be kind, for everyone you meet is fighting a hard battle."

vi) "Wonder is the beginning of wisdom."

About twenty-three hundred years ago from today, there was a country. The country was Greece. Born in present-day Europe, Socrates was a great man and a world-renowned philosopher. He is famous in the world today for the judgment he created. As the days go by he is becoming more relevant to the world. His two students, Plato and Xenophon, further exposed his ideology to the world in their writings. The ideology of his thought that started become magnificent in the world today.

What is that thought? What are its consequences? What is its ultimate consequence? What is the real truth? What is knowledge? How is it possible to improve human civilization?

He was the greatest proponent of the possible combination of science and philosophy. His thoughts still haunt people. Even if you just think about that day, everyone should be amazed.

We consider ourselves to be a modern and fortunate being possessed of a certain power. When you think about it, you think that you have a lot of knowledge. Everything that is created from the joy of life and therefore becomes the possessor of power forever.

Those of us who read a few books and think of ourselves as scholars open our eyes . Their intelligence should not be mixed with the wisdom. In many cases we all do that blunder. Some of the above statements are highlighted here. Everything we all know is a relative truth. What seems to be true today may change tomorrow in future context. A magical light of faith is constantly floating in front of our eyes. We can know a lot only by asking questions out of thirst for knowledge. We accept. Acceptance without question as true. The light of knowledge gives birth to various questions. So we should free ourselves from omniscient thinking. This idea only gives us that ignorance and arrogance. In this sea of knowledge, it is wise to give yourself new knowledge day by day. People constantly develop their thoughts and ideas, often intentionally or often unknowingly.

The introduction of Socrates' ideology has given birth to a timeless ideology. The matter is particularly noteworthy in this regard. So there is no place for self-satisfaction. You always have to learn and improve yourself. In no case should you indulge in self-indulgence. This stops the development of your preparation which is never desirable.

Explaining his ideology in this short range is nothing but foolishness. Everything is possible with a pure mind by clearing the garbage of the mind. Never think less of yourself than others. The future of those guilty of this is never good. They are left behind day after day. Deprived of the real joy of life from age to age.

Life is bright and promising. You make your own life. Conquer the thought again and again. Fly to the final stage. And so be it, the last smile is like you smile.

In a word, - "Socrates was a super human and he was ahead of age. Yes, he was even far more modern than that of today. He came to enlighten us and he purposefully did it with an unaltered way. History will definitely be amazed by his sacrifice. "

CHAPTER FIFTEEN

Morons: The ideal idle

There is a saying-"No pain no gain but I think there should be sufficiently gain without any type of pain."

This time is not as normal as other times. Infallible fence of rules all around. The people of the world are terrified. You may be wondering what is new again, we are all going through the same problem, there is peace all around, the environment is restoring its youth, new icebergs are appearing on the peaks of the mountains, the old birds seem to be in front of the people, As the level of environmental pollution decreases, forest dwellers are beginning to enjoy the environment of the past again. The world is beginning to find temporary protection from the tyranny of human beings. We have studied prehistoric data and found that nature does not tolerate anyone's oppression, nature obeys its own rules. In this way, many animals, birds and plants have become extinct from this world according to the infallible rules of time. This nature is not ours, we are the smallest part of nature. We are one of the millions of living and terrestrial species that live on earth, that is the human race or Homo sapiens. There is a class of people who discuss science day and night in an effort to make new discoveries for whom our way of life has reached its present stage. They don't like publicity at all. Our discussion today is not about these.

Our discussion today is about the people of that elite class who are going on strike and picketing in the paradise discussed in our mythology, who is not there? Their fear is that if an idiot goes to the after life in Covid-19 now, he will be freed from the service of one of the gods of the heavens. That is why Narada appears at the court of the Devaraja Indra, whose chances of losing his job is the largestest. Feeling the sense of danger, the Devaraja remembered the Tridev to save him from this great calamity.

The Tridev came and offered talks to understand the gravity of the danger, and when the Devadidev Mahadeb offered Narada to join the meeting as a special guest, the Brahma gladly accepted.

Peace was restored among the deities when the discussion was started among all the common deities. Since the Tridev did not have much information about the morons, the Chakradhari Bishnu necessarily allowed Narada to discuss the matter in detail.

After chanting his lord twice, Narada began to say the main thing.

The Morons will be both men and women. They think of yourself as omniscient, do not stop arguing about science even if you do not know science. Even if you are not proficient in fine arts and music, you will be ready to prove yourself proficient in those subjects. If they arrive in heaven, the Apsaras and Kinnaras will lost their job, they have to sit idle forever . If their music enters the ear channel, it will arouse your extreme humour, but the Tridev, you can't even laugh, lest they lose their self-esteem, Kinnaras will also be ready to discover new types of melodies and rhythms. O God! I have now tried to explain the reason for the strike of Kinnar and Apsara. I understood that, but why the Bishwakarma also? Said the Chakradhari.

Their brains will be very fertile. Even if you are not an expert in ecology, you will imagine big unrealities and if necessary, you will doubt the efficiency of ecologists and if necessary you will resort to lies and you will want to create public opinion by saying it in public to prove its information correctly. O God! It is a pity that many people will remain silent even after knowing everything and that is why morons will continue to get success one after another and their morale will continue to increase.

The Prajapita Bramha said "I understood it well, but O sage! Why are you so worried, I do not understand the reason?"

"I must be very worried, father" said Narada. They are better than me. I send huge amount of information from one deity, monster, Yaksha or Kinnara to another for the welfare of the world. O God best! The morons never think of this. They only think of their own gain and the loss of others. All the secrets of the other are easily told to the other, so that even if someone dies because of that, there will be no trace of affection in them, but they break the faith of the other and they prove those who believe in them as fools and do not hesitate to ridicule them. The secrets of their minds can be largely understood by looking them in the eye while talking to them. As a result, I know they are more skilled than I am. If so, where is the assurance of my job remain intact?

Besides, they are scientists, orators, philosophers, farmers, pastoralists, amphibians, nocturnal, foot-stealers, mosahebs, even dislikers of the Yama, what else?

Realizing this, the Devadidev Mahadev said, " This is also the end of my work." O Lord! Save us! Save us! Only the Brahma can do this. We all go to the remembrance of the Brahma at the same time. Saying this, everyone got up.

Then the Brahma said, "Don't worry, I don't want to disturb the peace here by bringing all these morons to heaven.Their world is the proper abode for them." Let them each develop in their own deeds and Narada, you will praise their deeds. In this work you have been specially appointed from today. I hope you have no objection now.

Listening to your hopes, some scientists in the world have been researching day and night in which the vaccine of Covid-19 has been discovered very soon and the arrival of morons in heaven will soon be stopped and the earth will return to its previous form.

Got it! Let us start another topic.

CHAPTER SIXTEEN

The child of Almighty

Every human being should always have a goal with which he makes his dream. His life revolves around this dream. He is always awake to fulfill it. Life without a goal is like a boat without oars and sails. Can't go on, So everyone's cooperation should always be sought. At this stage of life, everyone continues to move forward like a charm. Where is the problem then?

You will see that there is a class of people who never look for you, but they do not want you for your success at all. If you go to all these people sometime later, they all take advantage of your fragility equally. They do nothing to help you improve. In addition try to break your morale slowly with their versatile technique and stay behind you for a long time for watchthing. Never mind that they want the best for you! If you believe, you can check and see personally. You will see that step by step they are trying to harm you and keep you down which is particulaly not benefit for you and your much desired dream. A lot of the time your future depends on what you do then. Be a smart and take full advantage of your heart.

If you accept submission, that is your downfall. That's where all your efforts end. You are dead and they will all enjoy your condition like a charm. You will become a stagnant substance. One negligence game will start for you. You will sacrifice yourself like to all those morons. You are happy with it! Strange thing will started to follow.

People with spines will never be able to accept this. You will never have to accept your own insults. They will get up. That is why I will never do any tricks with these people at all. Only the fire of the mind will ignite behind everyone. You will move towards the goal with more perseverance by increasing the initiative. Then he will breathe only after reaching his desired goal. He wants to shout to the world, "I am not inferior to anyone. I am not neglected at all. I am also a child of Almighty. God also exists in me. I am equally important like everyone else. I have a beautiful mind like everyone else. I am also harsh and it hurts to be neglected. So don't despair if you can't help someone. It can take a lot of life and end a lot of time. "

CHAPTER SEVENTEEN

Constant effort: My success

"Relentless efforts in single direction is a key of every success"

One thing is for sure, many of us start thinking about a lot of things with a lot of energy in the beginning. I have been following it for quite some time in every case of my success. Many times I go quite a bit further. Then suddenly one day I left everything. Where is our effort lost? Many of us, as a result, cannot achieve the desired goal in time. Where do we get lost? This is a complete waste of our efforts, energy and time. We always lose to conscience. I can't look up in the mirror because of series of failure. We experience this in most cases. There are many reasons for this happenings. They were discussed gradually.

Many times our demand is met in a short time. For example, if a job seeker was first preparing for a job at the national level, the success rate of these was quite low. He was also giving many more low standard job exams at the same time. Since the standard of the exam is very high in the national arena, there is no doubt that he will always succeed in many job competitions before the candidates reach that level. Most of the time , he lost that zeal initially.

In the end, he was particularly satisfied with low expectation. This is particularly true in all kinds of people all over the world.

The ultimate lack of a long preparation mentality often deprives people of their desired benefits. Most people now want to succeed quickly. It is a mockery of success, I think. We all know there is no short cut in success. In no case, success could not be achieved through magic. Even so, owning one is still beyond the reach of the average person. As a result, I always get disappointing results. But most of the time it is seen that despite our ability we cannot achieve success.

Family unrest often hurts our efforts, greatly. In this case, the family members have to explain what is right and what is wrong for that candidate. When there is unrest in the mind, the final disturbance of attention occurs. Aa a result of which, we cannot pay full attention to our actions at all. We are then, bound to be failures.

A lot of times we become involved into some unwanted relationship which appears to be beneficial to the present context but detrimental to the future. Which never turn into profit in the future. Involvement in such a relationship is as detrimental to the health of the body and mind as it is detrimental to the individual's career or social status as a whole. It is true that some greedy people may benefit from this, but a class of people with simple beliefs repeatedly cheated. So if you have to help someone, never neglect yourself. Always think for yourself first. You have to take the policy otherwise you will always fall into trouble. Think in a little detail. In this world no one belongs to none. In this case, some people do not hesitate to perform heinous acts for their own interests. So it is very important to understand which is best suited for you. If you do not understand, there is a possibility of being deceived at every stage of life.

The example of Robert Bruce can be given in this case. Success will come at the door only if it is practiced at the tunes of highest level of purity of mind.

Nothing in the world is easily found or achieved. Success must be taken away or snatched. Nobody will give success as alms, you have to earn the success.

CHAPTER EIGHTEEN

Sixth Sense: Is it there?

"Inquisitive minds will find everything in the world one day. It was particularly true in the past, it is true in present and it will lead great role in the future even."

People should always abide by the reality. Can the results ever be better if you combine your life with an unreal story? This issue seems to be more controversial than real. This seemingly trivial matter can never be reconciled with reality. This is where the controversial situation arises. This is often called referred to as Sixth Sense. This Sixth Sense is very much confusing. It seems to me controversial and without any basic information. However, with a lot of past experience, it is possible to determine what will happen in the near future. This kind of sense does not seem to exist in a scientific way. Day by day, even if someone is doing something, it becomes termed as an experience not Sixth Sense.

The issue can often be considered as manifest in the case of non-human animals. In this case, it is deeply expressed. The five senses we have are eyes, ears, tongue, nose and skin. The perfect manifestation of the Sixth Sense is due to the harmonious combination of these five senses.

With these senses comes a strange combination of our brain. The greater the power of the brain of the person whose power of memory is greater.

Never mix sixth sense with it. Many claim that this has resulted in people protecting themselves from immediate danger. We do not know the actual result of it. Whether it is present or not is largely depend on the personal experience of the human beings. The inquisitive mind, however, cannot accept this .Sometimes it becomes utterly nonsense.

So may be or see a little more! This kind of nonsense can never be real without such controversy.

So even today, if we think of that strange thing as important, and become dependent on it, then we will often understand what the situation will be. Failure will be the only result there! Because Miracle does not happen all of a sudden. We have to make it happen.

CHAPTER NINETEEN

Failure of an individual: it's liability

"It simply came to our notice then that he was staying in same level for a long period. He was disappointed that he was not improving with the passage of time. His health was deteriorating day by day without any reason." Many people think so without thinking the obvious reason. This is almost always a common occurrence in everyday life among young students, including children in their teens. We all suffer from this issue more or less. Many of our relatives still suffer from such depression and after a long time like this a dark day comes down in their life. Many become mentally deranged again. Many unfortunate happenings are there because of this. Our loved ones have such misery in front of our eyes, we become observe this helplessly.

Many a time we are all shattered in our minds. This is Depression! So we have to remember that the graph of human life can never be one. The rise and fall of a living human being is inevitable and it is common to all. At least the survey says so. However, we can all improve the quality of this graph, if we think seriously so. If we want, we can restore the things we have lost in our lives quite easily.

Can get along better with people. Many times we can avoid sorrow and if we want we can free ourselves from being cheated. It is unfortunate that we ourselves often are not aware enough about our own talents. This is a situation where all the problems in the system start. Our society largely depends on the talent of the human beings. this is particularly true is all the situation we are facing day to day life.

Despair arises in this world only when we are unable to give any form of future direction to anyone. In order to give the right direction to this well-educated youth, there is a need for uniform thinking at all levels. Be it personal level, family level, and society level at large. Making a very important decision in this regard will ultimately benefit not only the person in question but the whole world. If we can sow such seeds of hope in a class of youth, then there will be a ray of hope to the future and a warm mentality among them so that they will be able to live their lives well together and many times social chaos will be prevented. This will ultimately beneficial to the whole world at large. So from the family level to the social level if we can think and apply it we can build a better society days to come.

So if we think deeply about the failure: then if any person fails then society cannot avoid its responsibility in any way. And if any society fails, who has ever thought of its responsibility? If a society fails, this is very much unfortunate to all person live in the society.

Thousands questions and information will come out when we start discussing this. But everyone has to think more and more about this. It is applicable for oneself, for society, for the country and above all for this world. The more meaningful we are, the more we will deliberately push ourselves forward. The country and the nation will prosper only if we think of the development of people from all walks of life. Never think of failure on a personal level. Failure of a person means failure of his family and above all society he or she lives.

Failure of an individual should not be considered at personal level. It should be considered as failure of society as a whole. This concept should be initiated to uplift the mental health of the mankind. We should not pretend to excuse us from those potential disasters that we have culminated over the years.

CHAPTER TWENTY

Success: The winning mantra

"World remembers the achiever only."

When a person reaches his desired goal, he has to accept various kinds of sacrifices, endure many insults and neglects and ignore many harsh words. Nature burns that person in different fires and turns him into a pure human being. Then he became a man of another nature.

The key to success is to look at the details in silence and very carefully. Besides, it is not necessary to involve oneself in all matters, otherwise all mental energy will not be concentrated. As a result, success will be delayed that is not desirable to any one.

Let me tell you a small story. It was 2005. We are then preparing for the competitive exam. I wrote my name and the word "Aspirant 2005" on the cover of one of my competitive books. The book was my own purchase. It was not supposed to be a problem for anyone. A few days later I saw "Aspirant 3005" written on the cover of that book. That is, "2" is replaced by "3". What a cruel, disgusting and silent joke! He knows it has happened in his case. Nothing can be said in the mouth in that case, even if the heart is burnt to ashes. If you want to protest verbally, he will say that he has written correctly! Your preparation not at all upto the mark to get a job after competition. So, it is better to remain silent and waiting for my turn.

I secretly criticized myself in details in my mind. This fact is very secrete no one knows. In my heart, I was shocked and devastated but I have to find a way out of it. After several days of thinking, I decided that in 2005 I would be successful. At least there is no other way.

After making such a decision, I personally changed my strategies, mainly two ways of work.

A) To stop wastage of time and proper use of time and elimination of unnecessary things.

I still adhere to it. If necessary, I use it in that time and keep on practicing again and again and always keep on discussing one thing in my mind. That's what stays in my head. At one time this was my world. That's what I was talking about. The whole time I was 100 percent immersed in that subject. I doubled my daily effective reading time. I remembered an indomitable and strange stubbornness. Thus the preparation reached an extreme. I was able to realize that in my mind.

B) Everything must be done unknowingly and secretly.

All such matters are very important and sensitive. So everything has to be done secretly. Otherwise, if the critics can understand your motif or mind, then they will resort to various tricks. In the end, it becomes even more difficult to fulfill. Different types of external forces take a stand against you. Many times you are embarrassed, the stress increases a lot of the time which is detrimental for your health and mind and also for your success.

With all these things in mind, I achieved the ultimate success in 2005 in two cases. I am working on one of them today. I believe, Your action should speak not words.

Uninterrupted hostility: My goodness

"An explained joke is no longer a joke." Voltaire

Adam got his first success that day. Naturally he is omnisciently happy. He told everyone about his success. If one succeeds after a lot of hardships, then one does not really have the knowledge of the direction. Then he would tell everyone about his happiness or success in his own way. We have not seen any crime in this. That is why he has become so overzealous in his open mind. See what happened! Let's analyze a little deeper.

Most of us have a laid back attitude when it comes to painting a picture about ourselves. This will cause many problems for many of us in the future. So if we think a little and step forward, many people can be saved from many dangers in the future.

As we can see from the details, the whole population always reacts to one thing in three ways.

1) Support - All these people can be divided into two ways again. With a little judgment we can analyze his reaction more thoroughly.

A) Support from the heart - All these people are simple and highly appreciate the success from the heart and encourage more for the future. Their body language is also very easy to understand.

B) Even if you say it orally, you do not support it from the heart - all these people are very complex in nature. Most simple people are deceived or have an extreme chance of being deceived. They are usually jealous. They are at the root of all the problems in this society. Almost all people misunderstand them and think of them as their friends. In a word, they are the black sheep. If you recognize them, stay away from them. Don't mess up them. They are opportunity seekers, they don't mess with anyone. This is their art. If you recognize such a person, stay away from him. In the end the benefit will be yours. They are secret enemies in the guise friendship.

2) Oppose - You easily recognize them. They are also simple. Since they are all easily identified, the result is better if you remove yourself from them. However, they do not secretly hostile. They also feel open hostility. Judging from the emotional side, they are open-minded. They can be easily recognised by understanding them with a little intellect.

3) Remains unresponsive - This class of people should be kept at a distance. Since they are also easily identified, the matter of their mental condition becomes easy for everyone to understand. However, many times the reason for being unresponsive is not easily understood. They are suspicious people and should be handled with utmost care.

One of the important things we can learn from the above is that most people don't happy about your success, but you can say a lot about yourself. By serving this joyful news, we unknowingly become the eyesore of some people. There is a proverb in ancient literature, "When happiness is shared, happiness grows." This is not true in all cases but in most cases it proves to be wrong. So understand yourself well and don't increase your trouble by starting unnecessary competition.

Besides, many people think it is foolish to share their private life publicly. It is wise also. Enjoy the joy of your own success in heart content and start a new chapter in life again. There is a wonderful saying "There is no enemy of deaf and dumb."

CHAPTER TWENTY-TWO

Work invisible to everyone

"Do not look back when you are leaving." Pythagoras

Nowadays people love to get a little publicity. Although it does not bring economic benefits, it often brings peace of mind. So almost everyone is promoting something without knowing it. In most cases during such propaganda we do not analyze the judgment of how it will affect us personally in the future. Do not discuss in a little detail! If your opponent knows what you are doing today, will it be good for you? The thinking mind does not want to accept any controversy. Really! Why would an intelligent person cut a canal and bring a crocodile? So you have to prepare for any work in silence. If it is invisible to everyone, there will be no obstacle from any direction.

There is no need to be stingy in all the preparations that have to be made for any work. There is no word - "No shield, no sword, Nidhiram Sardar"! In that case, your success will not come in any case. Always remember that every task is a battle. If you take it lightly at any time, you are bound to cheat. In each case, the plan is to move slowly and steadily. It takes a certain amount of time if we think this work is a big plan. People who climb the ladder of extra success divide all these big tasks into smaller ones. Then set small targets. In this way he continued his efforts. Day by day they surpass that small goal. They always stick to that goal. Then one day they reached their destination.

The method of reaching the goal by dividing this big goal into smaller ones is called Pomedoro method. This method is very important and useful.

The Pomodoro Technique was introduced in the late 1960's by the Italian philosopher Francesco Cirillo.

The word pomodoro is Italian, meaning tomato or eggplant. This method helps to easily remember any object or thing. The essence of Pomodoro Technique is already described above. We are not going to describe this technique in toto.

I myself am a big supporter of this method. I use this method not only to memorize the study, but also to reach the desired goal in other areas of life. There is constant evidence that one great achievement can be achieved by combining small successes. So you never have to stop the movement. The place of despair must be considered very important and responsible. Those frustrations, failures are also an integral part of life, it should never be forgotten. There is so much value in success because there are these, there is so much value in light because there is darkness. There is so much value in good because there is bad. So all the events that have taken place, there must be some causal relationship, if we discuss in a little detail and think deeply, everything will become clear like water.

CHAPTER TWENTY-THREE

First Impressions: It's effectivity

"Imagination is more important than knowledge"-Albert Einstein ."You never get a second chance to make the first impression," by Andrew Grant, a famous British writer.

Everytime when I myself very humble to the society for a particular reason to improve the society, some person take it as very easy and simply taken everything granted. I also found and face some undesirable situations that really disheartening to the society as a whole. Sometimes I become careless about it but it simply took a huge toll to me. Everytime such ignorance may harm a lot than making any good to you. So pay attention in such case. In case you are preparing for something, everytime come to public with proper dress. Knowingly or unknowingly you can reap a huge benefit from it. Even in case of attending office or other places, your first Impressions become very much beneficial for your immediate success. Don't ignore it. Your body language also plays a lot of role mainly during interview and such other important business. It is worthy to mention that not only your education but also immediate response to a particular situation play a lot of role during your way for future step. Your attitude and response towards a particular situation also play an important role in your heart and health also. So it also should not be taken lightly. Deep consideration and thoughtful mind during planning also plays an important role.

At the point of time, when you are trying to improve, everytime you should borne into mind that your outer apperance shall play an important role. We are sadly surrounded by majority of idiots who even don't know about themselves. So, they still belong to the that class who did not try to improve themselves everytime. It is really a pity.

Sometimes, unknowingly a few decisions are taken untimely which play important role for improvement. It should be handled with care.

Proper dress with good etiquette often won the race at the last. So care should be taken in this case. Simple or no use of brain is customary here which is matter of sorrow. So some high ranked people badly affected and took very bad decisions which ultimately become blunder for the society at large in long run.

Peer review status of the mankind, there is sadly no shortcut of success. Some cry in vain while some own the game alternatively.

It is very important to me but unfortunately I have received this message from the society. The rays of hope still there as all of you know that truth won at last of all and it is everlasting for the society.

It is astonishing that even the so called highly educated often fall in the prey of such first impression. So, I, often found it is not guilty to show off one's success in public. Everytime, often, the society looks your drape from toe to hair. So from shoe to hat, proper care should be taken during their choice. Often, one should thought every detail. Life is not a matter of gape and yawn. Take advantage it. Be serious, when times came. You will succeed, I am sure. Use your vibrant brain everytime. Love to download the energy that come to your way.

CHAPTER TWENTY-FOUR

The "Mother" method: An innovation

"I came, I saw, I conquered." - Napolean

Many of us have a laid back attitude when it comes to painting a picture about ourselves. I believe that if we think about all kinds of people, then the matter is quite confusing. There are many causal relationships on one subject. Each is equally important. So when it comes to answering or writing a question, there is a possibility of omitting a subject based reason. "This" mother "method is applied when answering so that no one is left out on the night of the affair. This method is a very urgent and simple method. I am the first author to use this method or technique. I have benefited a lot from using this method while taking part in competitive exams. It is easy to remember complex and confusing things. Using that method during the test, since we have to remember everything, they gladly give the test and they always give good results. It also makes the study much easier and simpler. The study became more exciting. The interest of students to study increases many times over.

In this way students should read the important points of the book well. Then the word "mother" must be formed with the first letters of all the root words of the causal relationship. Just remember the word "mother" during the test. The word "mother" is the cause of all actions because the words can be easily produced.

Giving an example will make the matter particularly clear.

Below, there are many ways to easily remember the work of the President of India. This is a particularly important and easily helpful way for students to remember.

Many of us know that the President of India has been given special powers. Those powers are, respectively,

1) Financial Power (F)

2) Administrative Power (A)

3) Legislative Power (L)

4) Emergency Power (E)

5) Judicial Power (Ju).

In this case the word "mother" is "FALEJU." This word is made up of one or more letters or alphabets from each topic. Everything is easy to remember if you remember the letters or alphabets. The more interesting the word "mother", the easier it will be to remember.

In order to remember the answers to the big questions, you have to make the words "mother" to your choice.

CHAPTER TWENTY-FIVE

Eureka Eureka

Today is the year 2022 A.D. The age of the earth is increasing day by day. Many new things have come to the fore. Many new things have been discovered so far. Scientists from different countries are still doing different kinds of work day and night. Many of their discoveries will bring about more changes during the days to come. We must always be ready for it and accept in open mind. The people who will welcome that change will reign forever. This is a proven fact. Those who do not readily accept the changes or reject that changes will perish day by day. We already witness such incidents in the history. The same thing will happen in the future. it will be a repetition of the past. It would not be otherwise. This was the case thousands of years ago, it is the same today and it will be the same in the future. There will be no change at all during all the ages to come.

Then we need to give the right direction to what this huge youth will keep in mind. It may seem like a very simple thing, but it is also very timely. We have to make this decision with a lot of thought. In this context, the most important thing we have to keep in mind is whether the society or the country wants anything from our work. If so, what is it? If we think deeply, we will get the right answer. Now if this desire matches our desire, then the matter becomes great.

How do we understand what the country or society wants? The answer is very straightforward. Now there are different types of vacancies in different types of newspapers and magazines. They need to be looked at very seriously. We all know about this. The problem that has arisen here recently is that there are many more job seekers than vacancy positions. As a result, we have to face a tough competition for this. This is a very good sign from the employer's point of view. He will get paid employees according to his choice. When you think of job seekers, one thing can be said - "But you need only one vacancy. Don't think too much. Make yourself more fit according to their choice. Never suffer form any complacency. Don't stop before you succeed. "

In this connection, it is necessary to introduce a small historical event. The name of the country is Greece and the person in question is Archimedes. The king of that country had a hobby of making a new crown. When it was made and brought to the king, many in the royal court began to doubt that it was pure gold. The king also had doubts in his mind that maybe the crown was not real gold. But who is the person who will accurately determine the purity of that crown? All the members of the assembly started asking and stare each other's faces. In the end, Archimedes was given that responsibility because his fame had spread country wide. Archimedes was also told that he could do no harm to the crown.

The next thing we're going to talk about is that the state always needs employees. This was also seen through this incident. What's more, we need the right person, not the wrong one. So the right people always have the right job.

He will be in the future a country.

Archimedes was very worried. Then while bathing in a pot full of water, he noticed that some water had overflowed and he also felt a little lighter. He decided that there must be a relation of density with this overflowing water. After the incident, he ran out into the street screaming "Eureka Eureka" or "I got it". As a result, he discovered buoyancy. This event is still remembered. in that way he discovered a new law of science. He accurately determined the purity of the crown and how adulterated it was.

It is true that not everyone is such a great scientist or a great man. But everyone has the potential to improve themselves even more. Many of us are taking advantage of that opportunity largely. Examples of such person are scattered all over our society. Failure will come. It is an integral part of everyone's life. So there is no place in life to be broken down. One day or another, every person will be successful and reign the world.

CHAPTER TWENTY-SIX

Common sense: Not common

"The best is yet to come." Frank Sinatra

Dynamics is a history in the history of human civilization for ages. There is a class of people who are working day and night without anyone noticing. Some of these people are unable to procure their own food and shelter. They procure their own food and shelter at the mercy of others. Another class of people is improving their lives day by day. Why is this happening? Why rich people are getting richer day by day, poor people are getting poorer!

Is there any injustice? If so, who is responsible? Whose fault is it? How can human society be saved from this? A detailed discussion of how poverty alleviation can be achieved by reducing premature deaths. It is not necessary to just discuss. A very necessary term plan is required for very local level to international forum. If you just pay for free, it will not come into reality at all. Yes, those who are physically disabled or crippled need to have separate bodies to take care of them separately and certain types of measure for check and balance should be initiated at once. It is not desirable for anyone to do any kind of work or plan, it should be fruitful and kind to human. In order to be accountable to humanity or conscience, one must come forward with an open mind. If you differentiate the plan without open mind and without proper planning, it will never work in the field. It should not be combined with other five or seven works that are not as important as their living. If you give something to someone easily, it is not appreciated, it will not be taken seriously. So before giving something to someone, you have to see if he deserves it! Otherwise ultimate results may be the opposite as desired during planning.

People say "Common sense is not at all common." We feel the matter during our work. It sounds very bad, but it's very important and sensitive. Many people do not understand his own well as well. In this case some intermediaries are created. They are good enough at frying fish in it's oil and use the benefits for their own well being. So to control them?. A class of people are deprived of it day after day. The more intermediaries there are like knowing a delivery, the more deprived the consumer will be. This is a proven fact.

Now let's talk about why the rich get richer day by day. People with foresight know how to plan fine and accurate! The big industrialists and businessmen, mainly on private initiative, continue to go ahead with such definite plans. They have a long-term definite goal. The bird's-eye view of the target continues to advance towards their goal. Since they are unwavering in their goals and their plans are unadulterated and they work tirelessly to achieve this goal day by day, they are also achieving the desired success in due time.

Ordinary people see only their success which become public. They may not even realize that they are working hard and planning day in and day out tirelessly. So as long as we reach out to the common people and discuss all these things in detail with them about the gravity and sustainability of planning and thus we will improve ourselves in such case the desired result bound to come.

Old-fashioned thinking should be replaced at once. It is not necessary to just discuss. You have to reflect on it at work. Even if there is a difference in words and deeds, all discussions will be meaningless and the poor become poor. It is the ultimate result. Sadly. this is true even in first world countries.

CHAPTER TWENTY-SEVEN

I am the best: The mental boost

Much does not depend on what the person thinks of himself in human life. In most cases, the person is not particularly confident about himself. Didn't discuss or criticize himself in detail. Tell me what others will think of him? What do you expect from others if you do not respect yourself? Something good, never! See yourself in an upstairs seat, learn to think. Change your gaze. Free yourself from those heartless thoughts, if necessary you have to change your partner instantly.

Behaviour changes very easily if you develop your own thoughts earlier. One has to restrain oneself from saying or doing what one suddenly does, like a person who has never thought before. Even the smallest decisions have to be made with a lot of thought. A wise decision that you take today can bring great benefits in the future. Our experience often helps us make this decision. You will notice, people accept a little bad thing easily! It is surprising to think that human beings do not easily understand the things suits him good. Remember, a bad decision always leads to bad results in the future. So a lot of time needs to be decided after prolong discussion.

At no point should you underestimate your self-esteem. As much as possible, avoid associating with people who do not show respect to others, no matter how great they may be. Talk less about it and get rid of it. The person who, no matter how dear you are, thinks you are cheap, is far from approaching him, stop talking or thinking about him. Our experience is that the more beautiful a person is, the more he develops physically and mentally. Make it a habit to be alone if necessary. The most important thing is that the basic condition of any basic thought is peace of mind. If there is no calm environment around, leave that place quitely. Make a habit of reading new books by giving up useless thought. Most people are stingy in collecting books. There is a little to think about the matter!

Students need to be confident in order to develop themselves as professionals. Lots of books to read with the mind. This book is man's greatest friend. If necessary, the stock of books should be increased. No scholar becomes a scholar by himself, behind him lies a lot of perseverance, a lot of sacrifice, a lot of hardship.

Don't go for less that your full potential. Change yourself first, not for others, for yourself, for your own benefit, for your own betterment, for a brighter future. Give yourself time, as if God Himself had to wait for that time. We all think badly about improving our lives, but not over time. The results are known to all. One should never go unintentionally to help or advise anyone. This can lead to two bad things. First, the person you love and want to help may not think you are important enough to make you feel humiliated. Secondly, you will not get any reward for it, in addition to the waste of your labour, time, money, you do not make a net profit, but a loss. And if you think it will one day benefit you unintentionally, then you are living in a fool's paradise. Get out of there now and be a realist and step on the ground of reality.

Hundreds of people have perished in this way, their families have been ruined. Their health has deteriorated, their minds are broken silently. It is foolish to think of those lucky people who have benefited today by being immersed in romance.

The more you can analyze yourself, the better. You just have to be more discriminating with the help you render toward other people. If necessary, the right decision should be taken at the right time by discussing how to improve all those aspects. It can become a better person. Don't give up, if someone else can do something, you can too. Think about it, maybe you can do better.

Remember the twentieth century was information technology or I. T Industry (Information Technology Industry) and 21st Century Data Industry (Data Technology).!

In this age of the Internet, information has become more accessible to all of us, so has the value of books diminished? Not at all, but the book has grown more and more day by day. Infrastructure has grown strangely in the last century. As a result, a lot of information or data has come from us. By analyzing all this information, we can guide the country more accurately. So our new direction has been unveiled. We can also use them to create something new. I can open new horizons and engage myself in writing new chapters.

Critics will criticize and condemn because this is normal, this is the natural law. This rule is no exception for you and me. In this case, you have to take yourself to such a height that the critics think thousands of times before criticizing. Let their heads be bowed in reverence. Let the pride of their knowledge be shattered to your personality.

You stand and remain like a rock both mentally and physically to achieve your goal. Iron determination is the only successful method. Be like that.

Developed world!: We dream it.

Tears came to my eyes today. What a cruel world! There is no form of mercy for the people of this world. There is a class of people who exploit innocent people day by day or use them in their work shamelessly. Throw them in the trash after use. Selfish people do not feel the need to inquire after that. Why? Their interests have already been achieved. They are engrossed in fulfilling any new interests. Those who are deceived, they are plunged into darkness by the opportunity of simplicity!

Do they have anything new to do! Yes, there is. There is so much to do. There is revenge. Have to prove yourself. There is a hint of turning around - in cheating. There is a hope for success. Step by step, something new can be created. If you express frustration, it will not happen. You don't want to bring someone you know back to life. He will come and increase your suffering. This will lead you to further destruction. Will be more damaged. Don't bow down to those heartless. Shout out with pride, I can live without you. I don't need you, I can do myself.

It's been a long time! I understand my importance. Everything in this world is fleeting. Now humanity has no place for these class of people. They can fool everyone with their subtle and efficient acting step by step. It takes a lot of work. After a few days, the truth came out. By then it was too late. Whoever is supposed to be the beneficiary, he can cross the line by then.

This is the real form of the developed world! Really impeccable. A group of masked people is flying towards victory, some candidates are always present in this situation. Always busy to flatter. History will not leave them alone. The common people will never get rid of all those candidates, flatterers, scoundrels in the speed of this age. Either they will sneeze or they will have to look red in the history of civilization. All of these things are so insignificant and trivial that you should never underestimate the importance of these details.

Think big if you can. Big, really big as large as you can. Think for the country. Think for the society. Leaving aside your own interests, think of something bigger that suit you better. You will see that the people around you are starting to look unfamiliar. Only then will you realize that you are on the right path. Overnight you will see how everything has changed. You are becoming much more universal. Many people are listening to you. You too are being considered as a guide.

Let's try something new in this world. Something good. Something improved. Something magnificient. Surely many people will see some light of hope in life.

Confidence: In mind

The main reason people are everywhere today is because of their self-confidence. The greater the self-confidence, the more it is always seen in his behaviour. He always does what he is told to do with confidence. This requires a smooth plan at all levels. Many people are needed in this situation. When planning, it is also important to decide who will execute the plan in the right environment at the right time. Otherwise, even with the right plan, there is no guarantee that the work will be completed properly. There is a need to pay close attention to this. It is equally important at the individual level and collectively.

On a personal level, this subject often helps him to win the victory of his own life.

Everything that has been discussed so far has been fine, then the problem arises when a person wants to suppress a particular person or class through his diplomacy! These can happen for many reasons No one will ever talk about such repression in the future. No one will ever admit it. Everything is done in secret and in terrible secrecy. In this case the mental zeal or self-esteem of that person or class is shattered with great care. They are humiliated in various ways, for some reason or another. Unnecessary questions were raised about their qualifications. Such a feeling is created by the conspiratorial point of views. As if, he can't do how to harm others. In most cases, the main conspirators remain unnoticed. Because if the matter becomes known, the life of that the prime suspect remains unnoticed. Although the matter is sad, it is widely discussed and become very much prevalent.

People with sharp intellects can catch those traps. Because their brains work a little more than others normal people. Besides, knowing that there was a personal conspiracy against him, Some of them made a lot of fun of it by pretending not to know about it. Dismanteling all those deep conspiracies, they started flying the victory flag of their own life. At the end of the day that conspirator fails miserably. By then it was too late. In this case, their end result is victory.

A small incident can be explained in more detail. The matter dates back to the English period British India. Stuart Lake was an English professor at a university. English was his subject. He let me write a letter one day. Everyone wrote the letter with their minds. He only looked at the books of Indian students. Looking at the notebook, he would say, "Indians can never write these things properly. They only know black magic."

Every time he insulted the Indian students in different ways. He would break the morale of Indian students in his mind. The reality was just the opposite. He knew that if Indian students were taught freely, many Indian scholars would be created. Which no British government would ever expect. So gradually all those meritorious students used to call the students as useless. Although it sounds bad, it is true that many incompetent natives used to support the British government in this work. Most of them do not understand the British properly.

It was going on like this. Mr. Lake wrote a letter to a talented local student one day. Then several months passed. Mr. Lake forgot about it. Suddenly one day he asked me to write the same letter again. The gifted student with magnificient knowledge wrote exactly what Mr. Lake wrote. What a surprise! Seeing that text, he said, "What a pity! There is so much wrong in this letter. There is no improvement for the Indians because of this."

After the incident, it became clear to everyone. No matter how well Indian students write, Mr. Lake would not have liked it. The real reason is that he did not like Indians. He never wanted the Indians to get the respect they deserved. So step by step he would hurt the self-esteem of the Indians breave hearts. His sole aim was to prevent the Indians from standing up to the British government with self-respect. Can't resist them. So gradually, in a scientific way, many British Indians would break their morale by hurting their self-esteem. He would crush them.

Well is that process used anywhere in present day ! There was a special request for everyone to think about the matter.

CHAPTER THIRTY

The living dead: Unfortunate

Yes! Life is so cruel. Many a time it is a blessing in disguise for us to let some people out of our lives. Because if they exist, life will not be good, but it becomes harmful day by day. Day by day they end their life lazily. Economic detriment, to the detriment of the social level. Even after that, if he is not removed from life, it causes such damage in the mind that the body becomes the home of many incurable diseases. Such people have a sharp intellect and are extremely magical. They are so poisonous that they can do great harm to any human being for their own short-term gain. He smiled very softly and talked and remembered. Usually they do not bring out their own nature. If that form ever comes out, save your life from danger by saying goodbye to him, no matter how dear you are. Never let self-satisfaction hinder you from improving your life. Living with all these poisonous people is like living with a poisonous snake. Again, if you think deeply, they are all even more harmful than snakes, because it is understood when a snake bites. He has treatment, but there is no guarantee that poisionus people will be harmed. When it is understood, it is too late. There is no way to do anything.

Without accepting. Again, it is difficult to accept from the mind. So if you are careful to have time, it is possible to avoid such unpleasant situations easily. In many cases the psychological damage is far greater than the economic damage. Many serious diseases have no shelter in the body. Many times your dearest or dearest person really immerses you in such an unpleasant environment. Many of us do not understand then what really should be done. Which way would it be better in the future?

Keep a cool head in this difficult situation. Do what you have to do. Learn to love yourself. Think of your parents. Work hard and do not not worry about your future. Give the reins of nonsense sky underground thoughts. Declare the person or persons who are causing such problems as dead. Otherwise you will be harmed. You will end up in a hurry. With that, your dream will end. How many hopes your parents have around you. Will they be implemented then?

It is very difficult to get out in such a healthy condition. Many times the mind is not willing to obey it instantly. After analysing the entire fact and circumstances, the right decision has to be made and that should be unaltered.

CHAPTER THIRTY-ONE

Eyes: Myth

"I'm almost forty years old. And like seven people, I can't play tricks. I'm the light in my parents' eyes. There's always a war going on in this world. Money is needed all the time. In the eyes of society, those who are successful are those who can make a lot of money. Either way! Is that to be considered? " I was thinking immortal in my mind and tears were falling in my eyes. For those for whom he gave almost all of his life except the soul of Dhar. Where are they today? Where was it not to happen? The day my parents were there, they were just arrogant and said we have money. Money is everything. We have no worries. Do what you think. He did not give due respect to any person. As a result, he is deteriorating day by day. What else happens in the life of the omniscient people!

What is arrogance in life? I do not understand anything. There is a class of people, they do not know what they think! The big ones are confused and arrogant. Do a little research, no one loves or respects them. They live in an illusory world. They have no contact with society.

Immortal falls asleep thinking about all this. Jane, his childhood friend, had been watching him for some time. They have grown together. Not married yet. She knew Adam very well. One day he came and took my hand and said: I am with you. "You always go through it, don't you want something for your life? I want it in your eyes. I don't see any time to think about it."

They never thought he would get such a life partner in so much sorrow. Liked him very much. How many days did he not read by himself while he was a student? Never ask him for any reward. It is better to say, never in these ways. That's it!

He just said in his mouth and in his heart he started thanking God. God is always with honest people. So no matter how hard it is, one should never give up the path of truth. The eyes of God are always on you. That vision is always auspicious.

He takes a vow in his mind, with God I have found myself, from now on I will not say anything and the world will see the result. Standing up again, I know the world well.

CHAPTER THIRTY-TWO

Holy December

Friends were rejoicing that day for some reason. 1ˢᵗ December in the calendar. World AIDS Day. That morning a huge truth in my life came before me. He is twenty-three and twenty-four years old. University student. I have gained a good reputation as a genius. I am participating in several job competitions. In most of the exams, I have crossed the boundaries of first and second stage. However, I have not got any job yet. I hope to get it in a few months. Smith in all these ways. He is a dear friend of mine.

So he had a dream about Anita. He did not say in the context of Anita! She was a student at our university. I liked her. Many dreams have been made about her in my mind. A lot of the time I would make future plans with her. I used to lie with her almost day and night. Everyone liked her mannerisms and manner of speaking. I didn't notice when that like turned into love and affection . I never told her that. But looking at her mannerisms, I could understand that Anita also likes me. That's how it went. I thought I would get a job and build a beautiful family in the near future. Husband and wife will both be educated. I will have a child. This is how I will spend my life. There is no limit to the spirits in the mind. That's how it goes day after day. I could not hold the emotions of the mind. So I told the story to a dear friend. They are very happy. Why not?

They said make the relationship solid so that you can pay more attention to your studies. After much thought, I said their words one day. The day is the 1st of December. Anita became like hearing the word! She said come in the afternoon and also requested "Please come alone".

What happens! I came alone in the afternoon according to her words. In front of her hostel. I see tears falling from her eyes rolling through cheeks. It's as if the throat has been choked. It can be seen that it is severely damaged. She said, "Listen! never try to come in front of me again. What you have planned will not come into reality. This cannot happen." She almost ran away. It was as if the matter was over before I realized it. What happened? I realized at night. No more sleep. I could not eat for a few days. Vomiting. Only a broken dream, tears with two eyes. Once I thought, what is the benefit of living a failed life? Then I remember my parents and loved ones. Changed the decision instantly.

How many hundreds of competitive exams ahead. Sometimes later, I forgot everything and focused on my studies. I promised in my heart, I will live as one. Yet only tears flow with two eyes. The mind does not want to obey. The matter was so secreate, can not ventilate either.

I went in this condition for several days. A few friends. I think I could feel it. They almost crack joke and say when to feast!

Meanwhile, after a few days, my mind became more stubborn. I made a firm promise in my mind- "I shall succeed, I will be an officer in the most prestigious department of the state. I will prove that the decision she has taken to leave me would be wrong. I will prove to myself for myself. I was the best, I am the best and I will be the best."

Whatever you think, work to everyone's surprise, Smith, after sometime, was appointed to the highest office in the state that year. That instant year.

Friends and acquaintances were then seen to say- "Whatever you are touching is now turning to gold. What is the key to this success?"

It was great to see everyone happy. All sorrow is now over. Today I have enough money, honour, car and house in hand. One by one the dream has come into reality. In fact, to enjoy life today!

But in my mind that broken dream is still shaken like a light breeze. There is everything in life except her. So even today when Smith thinks about Anita, there is a feeling inside his heart. Maybe an unexpressed pain maybe something else.

The stubborn Smith still doesn't want anyone to know about Anita's news and doesn't even want to try to get any news about her because her Anita is dead. The day of death is the 1st of December. But Anita may still be hidden in her heart as a memory across a small place. Maybe a happy memory or intense hatred.

CHAPTER THIRTY-THREE

Wise, be thee

Every creature is born and grows up in the pure love of the world. Is nurtured. From the unicellular amoeba to the most complex multicellular human being, this nature gradually grows from small to the infinite grace of the mother. In childhood, every animal nurtures its helpless child according to the simple rules of nature. Then came the ruthless struggle.

That is why human society is considered the best. It is seen that one class of people easily moves slowly towards the peak of improvement day by day. The progress of another class of people is not so fast. It takes a long time. His cause analysis began long ago. The German scientist William Stern elaborated on this in his book. The method by which he measures human intelligence is called Intelligence Coefficient (I.Q). It is measured in percent. Its mean is one hundred (100) and standard deviation is fifteen (15)! That is, the value of the common man will be eighty-five (85) to one hundred and fifteen (115). As people are improving day by day, so has the quality and development. That's normal. This is a proven fact. This is called Flynn Effect. Its growth rate is close to three percent in a decade.

In this way the answer to why the younger generation is wiser than the older ones is found. This is a proven fact. The higher the IQ, the faster he can grasp and remember. That is why the success of that person comes so quickly. That's why some people will see the face of success in less time. It's a lot of human genetics. It also depends on the education of the parents, the environment and the daily diet. So you should always eat a balanced diet.

As the days go by, new ideas are coming in the way. Scientists were watching the high I.Q. People with high I.Q. often can't do a lot of work successfully, but some common man can perform the works very efficiently. The person with the normal intelligence could do that easily. There was no scientific explanation for this. It was seen that some emotional people easily completed all these tasks with the help of others. The passion of all these people to speak could bring extreme faith in the minds of the listeners. As a result, big work was being done effortlessly. The emotions of those speakers were responsible for this. Keith Beasley was the first to give a good answer. He came up with a kind of information called Emotional Quotient (E.Q.). In this case, the person who can do the necessary work by controlling the emotions of others as needed is considered a person with a high emotional quotient. They are very successful as a leader of any organization. They know that any work can be done easily with any person. As a result, their future plans are very good. In this tradition all the millionaires are strong in this strange power. Each of all millionaires, the E.Q. are usually too high.

In 1995, Daniel Goleman discussed in detail his book Emotional Intelligence (E.I.). The book also won the title of Best Selling. He then gave detailed information on how to measure it in his book. This thrilling book has easily solved many complex questions. Less educated people than well-educated people are often known as good teachers. This is because he taught the students with passion and compassion. In this case, the study is often good, they get good results because they can be united with that teacher. Also the study is of much better quality as a result. Which is desirable for all students. This means that there is no guarantee that he will study with compassion even if he is highly educated. This is evidenced by the emotional quotient (E.Q.) of the active I.Q. often higher. The emotional quotient often less in highly educated person than of the less educated person . However, the opposite also may be true.

In today's world, even the most complex relationship, including the buyer-seller relationship, can be easily analyzed with these two issues. Government and non-government organizations often provide various types of training in this regard. As a result, people trained in training workshops are often seen to be established in their own field. Such benefits are often seen hand in hand.

Jack Ma, the current founder of Alibaba in China, first came up with the idea of Love Quotient (L.Q.). By this he has proved that public dealing or social communication is often done better by people than machines. Also, people who get along well with everyone, their business goes well and their future is bright. He can easily take the initiative to grow his company day by day with the help of his skills. These small things often pay off in the long run.

The new ideas that have emerged in the advanced social system are the result of many studies. These are tested and established as true. So as much as we can accept them without argument, they will be helpful for the development of our society and people. This will create new big companies, new rich people, new societies and new classes of people. Our hope is that the new society will show a new direction to the people of the world in economic, social, cultural, entertainment and above all in all fields.

In this context, all those quotes are no more.

CHAPTER THIRTY-FOUR

The fruit: The faith: The words

Man is a strange creature. This world has an important role to play. Humans are the best creatures in the world. All other creatures and plants accept human submission. Humans are the only animals they lie to. Blaming others. Hides one's own faults or mistakes. This is the basic human instinct. The more intelligence a person has, the more skill he has. That's normal. It depends a lot on the values of the society in which the person grew up, the values of the parents.

People can lie, cheat, kill or deceive. Knows how to lie. It has been seen that everyone lies. But who will say how much depends on his values. It has nothing to do with higher education. But there are definitely higher values. People basically accept the situation as a lie. It has also been observed that people lie at different times. They are sometimes fearful, sometimes violent. There could also be many more reasons.

So when people are telling the truth is very controversial. That or those who say - "It is a sin to lose faith in people." I personally strongly oppose it. People want to tell lie, people are talkative, lazy. People are born and grow up with these bad qualitiess. Human's affection, imparting proper education and training and frees the people from all such evil qualities.

So it is foolish to believe a stranger in the first instances. He should be believed only by observing his conduct and deeds, otherwise he may be terribly deceived which is not desirable. A person's assessment of another third person is never accurate, nor can it be. Because it is nothing more than relative. However, there are many loose control systems for people from all walks of life. I do not know how scientific they are?

How many people there are, they just earn by cheating other people and make a living. There are some professions that have no scientific explanation but almost everyone has come to believe it day after day. Day after day, with the help of that false belief, one class of people is exploiting them day after day on the pretext of their own cleverness and another class of ignorance. Think about it! What a terrible lie!

Humanity is at it's stake. What a cruel joke, that is!. It takes time to be faithful. Not everyone is faithful. So improved generosity of mind and fidelity should not be expected from everyone.

I remembered a line in that context,

"Not present, that's why you're sitting and taking advantage

If so present where to get such advantage.

Says the poet Kalidasa

while on the road. "

Although riddled, the matter is quite interesting. The point is, word of mouth. This is a cow's soliloquy. The cow has no tail. In such a situation, a fly is sitting on his body and irritating him. Then the cow is angry and says this to the fly.If the tail was there, he would kill the fly.

Liars are tricky and used to play hide and seek game; That too with great cunning. They do not lie but weave an incomprehensible magic in everything. Many people become involved in magic in the end and was defeated at the end.

But not without hope. I hope that the conduct of most of the people in a fully educated society is elegant and polite. There must be truthful people and they still hold such a high position in the society that it is good for all people. So ordinary people still live in peace. They have always been working for the society and the people.

A country can only prosper when it considers values to be the most important thing.

Values are the key to every success of the society. It is priceless.